POCKET PRAYERS

Pocket Prayers

COMPILED BY
Christopher Herbert

CHURCH HOUSE
PUBLISHING

Church House Publishing
Church House
Great Smith Street
London SW1P 3NZ
Tel: 020 7898 1451
Fax: 020 7898 1449

ISBN 0 7151 4039 6

Published 1993 by The National Society and
Church House Publishing

Typeset by Vitaset, Paddock Wood, Kent
Printed in England by the University Printing Press,
Cambridge

CONTENTS

To my wife Jan
for her wisdom, astringent
common sense and loving kindness
over the years

INTRODUCTION

Ever since life began people have felt the need to pray. They have sensed that God listens and they have found that the more they have prayed, the more they have discovered about God, other people and themselves.

Over the centuries certain prayers have been written down because they captured what we all want to say but have been unable to express for ourselves.

Here is a collection of prayers which have stood the test of time; prayers to rely on when our own words fail; prayers to take us close to the heart of God.

+ Christopher Herbert
  Bishop of St Albans

THE LORD'S PRAYER

Our Father, who art in heaven,
hallowed be thy name;
thy kingdom come;
thy will be done;
on earth as it is in heaven.
Give us this day our daily bread.
And forgive us our trespasses,
as we forgive those who trespass against us.
And lead us not into temptation;
but deliver us from evil.

For thine is the kingdom, the power,
    and the glory,
for ever and ever. Amen.

*

THE JESUS PRAYER

Lord Jesus Christ, Son of God,
have mercy on me, a sinner.

CONTEMPORARY VERSION

Our Father in heaven,
hallowed be your name,
your kingdom come,
your will be done,
on earth as in heaven.
Give us today our daily bread.
Forgive us our sins
as we forgive those who sin against us.
Lead us not into temptation
but deliver us from evil.

For the kingdom, the power,
and the glory are yours
now and for ever. Amen.

THE GRACE

The grace of our Lord Jesus Christ,
and the love of God,
and the fellowship of the Holy Spirit,
be with us all evermore. Amen.

ADORATION

You are worthy, O Lord our God, to receive glory and honour and power, because you created all things; by your will they were created and have their being!

Revelation 4.11

*

Glory be to the Father, and to the Son, and
    to the Holy Spirit:
As it was in the beginning, is now,
    and ever shall be, world without end.
    Amen.

*

Great and marvellous are your deeds,
O Lord God, sovereign over all;
Just and true are your ways,
O King of the ages.
Who shall not fear you, Lord,
    and do homage to your name?
For you alone are holy.
All nations shall come and worship
        before you, for your just decrees
        stand revealed.

Revelation 15.3-4

✳

We praise thee, O God: we acknowledge
thee to be the Lord.
All the earth doth worship thee: the Father
everlasting.
To thee all Angels cry aloud: the Heavens,
and all the Powers therein.
To thee Cherubin, and Seraphin:
continually do cry.
Holy, Holy, Holy: Lord God of Sabaoth;
Heaven and earth are full of the Majesty of
thy glory.

From the Te Deum Book of Common Prayer (1662)

*

O come, let us worship God our king,
O come, let us worship and fall down
before Christ, our king and our God.
O come, let us worship and fall down
before the very Christ, our king and
our God.
O come, let us worship and fall down
before him.

Liturgy of St John Chrysostom (4th century)

O Father, give the spirit power to climb to the fountain of all light, and be purified. Break through the mists of earth, the weight of the clod. Shine forth in splendour, thou that art calm weather and quiet resting place for faithful souls. To see thee is the end and the beginning. Thou carriest us, and thou dost go before. Thou art the journey and the journey's end.

Boethius (480–524)

My whole heart I lay upon the altar of thy praise, an whole burnt-offering of praise I offer to thee. Let the flame of thy love set on fire my whole heart, let nought in me be left to myself, nought wherein I may look to myself, but may I wholly burn towards thee, wholly be on fire towards thee, wholly love thee, as though set on fire by thee.

St Augustine (354–430)

Let all the world in every corner sing,
My God and King!
The heavens are not too high,
His praise may thither fly;
The earth is not too low,
His praises there may grow.
Let all the world in every corner sing,
My God and King!

George Herbert (1593–1632)

God, great and wonderful, who hast created
the heavens, dwelling in the light and
beauty thereof, who hast made the earth,
revealing thyself in every flower that opens;
let not mine eyes be blind to thee, neither
let mine heart be dead, but teach me to
praise thee, even as the lark which offereth
her song at daybreak.

St Isidore of Seville (560–636)

The almighty Truth of the Trinity is our Father, for He made and sustains us; the deep Wisdom of the Trinity is our Mother, in whom we are all enfolded; the great Goodness of the Trinity is our Lord; in Him we are enfolded and He in us. We are enfolded in the Father, and we are enfolded in the Son and we are enfolded in the Holy Spirit. The Father is enfolded in us, and the Son is enfolded in us, and the Holy Spirit is enfolded in us: All-mighty, All-wisdom, All-goodness: one God, one Lord.

Julian of Norwich (1342–1413)

CONFESSION

If we claim to be sinless, we are self-deceived and the truth is not in us. If we confess our sins, God is just and may be trusted to forgive our sins and cleanse us from every kind of wrongdoing.

1 John 1.8-9

＊

O Lamb of God
that takest away the sins of the world
have mercy upon us.

O Lamb of God
that takest away the sins of the world
have mercy upon us.

O Lamb of God
that takest away the sins of the world
grant us thy peace.

＊

Lord have mercy upon us.
Christ have mercy upon us.
Lord have mercy upon us.

❋

Almighty and most merciful Father;
We have erred, and strayed from thy ways
like lost sheep. We have followed too much
the devices and desires of our own hearts.
We have offended against thy holy laws.
We have left undone those things which we
ought to have done; And we have done
those things which we ought not to have
done; And there is no health in us.
But thou, O Lord, have mercy upon us,
miserable offenders. Spare thou them,
O God, which confess their faults. Restore
thou them that are penitent; According
to thy promises declared unto mankind in
Christ Jesu our Lord. And grant, O merciful
Father, for his sake; That we may hereafter
live a godly, righteous, and sober life,
To the glory of thy holy name. Amen.

Book of Common Prayer (1662)

Saviour of the world, the son Lord Jesus:
    stir up thy strength and help us,
    we humbly beseech thee.
By thy cross and precious blood thou hast
    redeemed us: save us and help us,
    we humbly beseech thee.
Thou didst save thy disciples when ready to
    perish: hear us and save us,
    we humbly beseech thee.
Let the pitifulness of thy great mercy loose us
    from our sins, we humbly beseech thee.
Make it appear that thou art our Saviour
    and mighty deliverer: O save us that we
    may praise thee, we humbly beseech thee.
Draw near according to thy promise from
    the throne of thy glory: look down and
    hear our crying, we humbly beseech thee.
Come again and dwell with us, O Lord
    Christ Jesus: abide with us for ever,
    we humbly beseech thee.
And when thou shalt appear with power
    and great glory, may we be made like
    unto thee in thy glorious kingdom.
Thanks be to thee, O Lord.
Alleluia! Amen.

The Daily Office (1968)

We do not presume to come to this thy Table, O merciful Lord, trusting in our own righteousness, but in thy manifold and great mercies. We are not worthy so much as to gather up the crumbs under thy Table. But thou art the same Lord, whose property is always to have mercy: Grant us therefore, gracious Lord, so to eat the Flesh of thy dear Son Jesus Christ, and to drink his Blood, that our sinful bodies may be made clean by his Body, and our souls washed through his most precious Blood, and that we may evermore dwell in him, and he in us. Amen.

Book of Common Prayer (1662)

*

Lord, for thy tender mercies' sake, lay not
our sins to our charge, but forgive that
which is past and give us grace to amend
our lives; to decline from sin and incline
to virtue, that we may walk with a perfect
heart before thee, now and evermore.

Bishop Ridley's Prayers (1566)

＊

Almighty and everlasting God, who hatest
nothing that thou hast made, and dost
forgive the sins of all them that are penitent:
Create and make in us new and contrite
hearts, that we worthily lamenting our sins,
and acknowledging our wretchedness, may
obtain of thee, the God of all mercy, perfect
remission and forgiveness; through Jesus
Christ our Lord. Amen.

Book of Common Prayer (1662)
(but dating from the 7th century or earlier)

＊

Drop thy still dews of quietness
Till all our strivings cease;
Take from our souls the strain and stress
And let our ordered lives confess
The beauty of Thy peace.

John Greenleaf Whittier (1807–92)

＊

Almighty God, Spirit of purity and grace,
in asking thy forgiveness I cannot
claim a right to be forgiven but
only cast myself upon thine
unbounded love.
I can plead no merit or desert:
I can plead no extenuating circumstances:
I cannot plead the frailty of my nature:
I cannot plead the force of the temptations
I encounter:
I cannot plead the persuasions of others
who led me astray:
I can only say, for the sake of Jesus Christ
thy Son, my Lord. Amen.

John Baillie (1886–1960)

Almighty God, our heavenly Father,
   we have sinned against you and against
   our fellow men,
in thought and word and deed,
through negligence, through weakness,
through our own deliberate fault.
We are truly sorry
and repent of all our sins.
For the sake of your Son Jesus Christ,
   who died for us,
forgive us all that is past;
and grant that we may serve you in
   newness of life
to the glory of your name. Amen.

Alternative Service Book 1980

THANKSGIVING

Praised be the God and Father of our Lord Jesus Christ! In his great mercy by the resurrection of Jesus Christ from the dead, he gave us new birth into a living hope, the hope of an inheritance, reserved in heaven for you, which nothing can destroy or spoil or wither.

1 Peter 1.3-4

*

My soul doth magnify the Lord: and my
    spirit hath rejoiced in God my saviour.
For he hath regarded: the lowliness of his
    hand-maiden.
For behold from henceforth: all generations
    shall call me blessed.
For he that is mighty hath magnified me:
    and holy is his name.

From the Magnificat
Book of Common Prayer (1662)

*

O all ye works of the Lord, bless ye the
Lord: praise him and magnify him
for ever.
O ye angels of the Lord, bless ye the Lord:
praise him and magnify him for ever.
O ye children of men, bless ye the Lord:
praise him and magnify him for ever.
O ye servants of the Lord, bless ye the Lord:
praise him and magnify him for ever.

From the Benedicite
Book of Common Prayer (1662)

*

Thanks be to thee,
    O Lord Jesus Christ,
For all the benefits
    which thou hast won for us,
For all the pains and insults
    which thou hast borne for us.
O most merciful Redeemer,
Friend and Brother,
May we know thee more clearly,
    love thee more dearly,
    and follow thee more nearly,
    day by day.

Richard of Chichester (1197–1253)

＊

I can do nothing
for my family
for people
or the Lord.
For the abundant love
of the Lord
of people
of my family
I just give thanks
just give thanks.

Mizuno Genzo (20th century)

Thou who hast given so much to me
Give one thing more, a grateful heart,
For Christ's sake.

George Herbert (1593–1632)

Blessed are you, Lord, God of all creation. Through your goodness we have this bread to offer, which earth has given and human hands have made. It will become for us the bread of life.

Blessed are you, Lord, God of all creation. Through your goodness we have this wine to offer, fruit of the vine and work of human hands. It will become our spiritual drink.

The Sunday Missal

✳

Almighty God, Father of all mercies, we thine unworthy servants do give thee most humble and hearty thanks for all thy goodness and loving-kindness to us, and to all men; we bless thee for our creation, preservation, and all the blessings of this life; but above all, for thine inestimable love in the redemption of the world by our Lord Jesus Christ; for the means of grace, and for the hope of glory. And, we beseech thee, give us that due sense of all thy mercies, that our hearts may be unfeignedly thankful, and that we shew forth thy praise, not only with our lips, but in our lives; by giving up ourselves to thy service, and by walking before thee in holiness and righteousness all our days; through Jesus Christ our Lord, to whom with thee and the Holy Ghost be all honour and glory, world without end. Amen.

Book of Common Prayer (1662)

Father of all, we give you thanks and praise, that when we were still far off you met us in your Son and brought us home. Dying and living, he declared your love, gave us grace, and opened the gate of glory. May we who share Christ's body live his risen life; we who drink his cup bring life to others; we whom the Spirit lights give light to the world. Keep us firm in the hope you have set before us, so we and all your children shall be free, and the whole earth live to praise your name; through Christ our Lord. Amen.

Alternative Service Book 1980

✳

REQUESTING

Marana tha – Come, Lord!

1 Corinthians 16.22

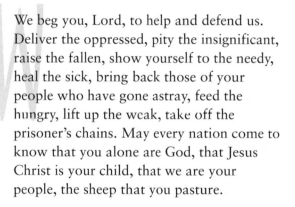

We beg you, Lord, to help and defend us. Deliver the oppressed, pity the insignificant, raise the fallen, show yourself to the needy, heal the sick, bring back those of your people who have gone astray, feed the hungry, lift up the weak, take off the prisoner's chains. May every nation come to know that you alone are God, that Jesus Christ is your child, that we are your people, the sheep that you pasture.

St Clement of Rome (d. AD 95)

Almighty God, bestow upon us the meaning of words, the light of understanding, the nobility of diction and the faith of the true nature. And grant that what we believe we may also speak.

St Hilary (315–67)

*

Eternal God,
the light of the minds that know thee,
the joy of the hearts that love thee,
the strength of the wills that serve thee;
grant us, so to know thee that we may truly
    love thee,
so to love thee that we may freely serve thee,
whose service is perfect freedom,
through Jesus Christ our Lord.

Gelasian Sacramentary (7th century)

*

Almighty God, who hast given us grace at
this time with one accord to make our
common supplications unto thee; and
dost promise, that when two or three are
gathered together in thy Name thou wilt
grant their requests: Fulfil now, O Lord,
the desires and petitions of thy servants,
as may be most expedient for them;
granting us in this world knowledge
of thy truth, and in the world to come
life everlasting.

Book of Common Prayer (1662)
Prayers of St Chrysostom (Byzantine Liturgy)

✳

O gracious and holy Father,
give us wisdom to perceive thee,
intelligence to understand thee,
diligence to seek thee,
patience to wait for thee,
eyes to behold thee,
a heart to meditate upon thee
and a life to proclaim thee:
through the power of the spirit of
Jesus Christ our Lord.

Attributed to St Benedict (480–543)

Lord Jesus Christ, who didst choose thine
apostles that they might preside over us as
teachers: may it also please thee to teach
our bishops who serve in the place of thine
apostles, and so to bless and instruct them
that they may be preserved unharmed and
undefiled in all their ways for evermore.

Egbert, Archbishop of York (d. 766)

We bring before Thee, O Lord,
the troubles and perils of peoples and
    nations,
the sighings of prisoners and captives,
the sorrows of the bereaved,
the necessities of strangers,
the helplessness of the weak,
the despondency of the weary,
the failing powers of the aged.
O Lord, draw near to each,
for the sake of Jesus Christ our Lord.

St Anselm (1033-1109)

*

O heavenly Father, the Father of all wisdom,
understanding and true strength, send thy
Holy Spirit into our hearts; that when we
must join the fight in the field for the glory
of thy holy name, we may manfully stand
strengthened by thee in the confession of
thy faith and of thy truth to our life's end;
through Jesus Christ our Lord.

Nicholas Ridley (1500–55)

O Divine Master,
grant that I may not so much seek
to be consoled as to console,
to be understood, as to understand,
to be loved, as to love,
for it is in giving that we receive,
it is in pardoning that we are pardoned,
and it is in dying that we are born
to eternal life.

Attributed to St Francis of Assisi (1182–1226)

*

Lord, make me an instrument of thy peace,
where there is hatred, let me sow love;
where there is injury, pardon;
where there is discord, union;
where there is doubt, faith;
where there is despair, hope;
where there is darkness, light;
where there is sadness, joy;
for thy mercy's sake.

Attributed to St Francis of Assisi (1182–1226)

Give me, O Lord, a steadfast heart, which
no unworthy thought can drag downwards;
an unconquered heart, which no tribulation
can wear out; an upright heart, which no
unworthy purpose may tempt aside.
Bestow upon me also, O Lord my God,
understanding to know thee, diligence
to seek thee, wisdom to find thee, and a
faithfulness that may finally embrace thee;
through Jesus Christ our Lord.

Thomas Aquinas (1225–74)

✳

O Lord Jesus, let not thy word become a
judgement upon us, that we hear it and do
it not, that we know it and love it not, that
we believe it and obey it not; thou who with
the Father and the Holy Spirit livest and
reignest, world without end.

Thomas à Kempis (1379–1471)

✳

Grant to me, O Lord, to know what I ought to know, to love what I ought to love, to praise what delights thee most, to value what is precious in thy sight, to hate what is offensive to thee. Do not suffer me to judge according to the sight of my eyes, nor to pass sentence according to the hearing of the ears of ignorant men; but to discern with true judgement between things visible and spiritual, and above all things to enquire what is the good pleasure of thy will.

Thomas à Kempis (1379–1471)

✳

The things, good Lord, that we pray for,
give us grace to work for;
through Jesus Christ our Lord.

Thomas More (1478–1535)

✳

Let nothing disturb thee,
Let nothing dismay thee:
All things pass:
God never changes.
Patience attains
All that it strives for:
He who has God
Finds he lacks nothing:
God alone suffices.

St Teresa of Avila (1515–82)

*

Ah, dearest Jesus, holy Child,
Make thee a bed, soft, undefiled
Within my heart, that it may be
A quiet chamber kept for thee.

Martin Luther (1483–1546)

*

Take, Lord, and receive all my liberty, my memory, my understanding, and my entire will, all that I have and possess. Thou hast given it all to me. To thee, O Lord, I return it. All is thine, dispose of it wholly according to thy will. Give me thy love and thy grace, for this is sufficient for me.

Ignatius of Loyola (1491–1556)

Most gracious Father, we most humbly beseech thee for thy Holy Catholic Church. Fill it with all truth; in all truth with all peace. Where it is corrupt, purge it; where it is in error, direct it; where anything is amiss, reform it; where it is right, strengthen and confirm it; where it is in want, furnish it; where it is divided and rent asunder, make up the breaches of it, O thou Holy One of Israel.

William Laud (1573–1645)

Lord, help me to know that:
He who is down need fear no fall,
He that is low, no pride;
He that is humble, ever shall
Have God to be his guide.
Make me content with what I have
Little be it or much;
And, Lord, contentment ever crave,
Because thou savest such.

John Bunyan (1628–88)

O eternal wisdom instruct me,
O eternal light illuminate me,
O eternal purity cleanse me,
O thou omnipresent power strengthen me,
O infinite holiness sanctify me,
Immutable love establish me,
Eternal mercy have mercy on me.

Thomas Traherne (1637–74)

O God, make the door of this house wide enough to receive all who need human love and fellowship, and a heavenly Father's care; and narrow enough to shut out all envy, pride, and hate. Make its threshold smooth enough to be no stumbling-block to children, nor to straying feet, but rugged enough to turn back the tempter's power: make it a gateway to thine eternal kingdom.

Thomas Ken (1637–1711)
(At the door of a Christian hospital)

✳

O God, help us not to despise or oppose what we do not understand.

William Penn (1644–1718)

✳

O Lord our heavenly Father, Almighty and everlasting God, who hast safely brought us to the beginning of this day; Defend us in the same with thy mighty power; and grant that this day we fall into no sin, neither run into any kind of danger; but that all our doings may be ordered by thy governance, to do always that is righteous in thy sight; through Jesus Christ our Lord. Amen.

Book of Common Prayer (1662)
(but dating from the 7th century or earlier)

O Lord, thou knowest how busy I must be this day; if I forget thee, do not thou forget me; for Christ's sake.

General Lord Astley (1579–1652)
(before the battle of Edgehill)

Lighten our darkness, we beseech thee,
O Lord; and by thy great mercy defend
us from all perils and dangers of this night;
for the love of thy only Son, our Saviour,
Jesus Christ. Amen.

Book of Common Prayer (1662)
(but dating from the 8th century or earlier)

❋

Almighty God, give us grace that we may
cast away the works of darkness, and put
upon us the armour of light, now in the
time of this mortal life, in which thy Son
Jesus Christ came to visit us in great
humility; that in the last day, when he shall
come again in his glorious Majesty to judge
both the quick and the dead, we may rise
to the life immortal, through him who
liveth and reigneth with thee and the Holy
Ghost, now and ever. Amen.

Book of Common Prayer (1662)
(but dating from the 7th century or earlier)

❋

Make me remember, O God, that every day is your gift and ought to be used according to thy command, through Jesus Christ our Lord.

Samuel Johnson (1709–86)

Incline us, O God! to think humbly of ourselves, to be saved only in the examination of our own conduct, to consider our fellow creatures with kindness, and to judge of all they say and do with the charity which we would desire from them ourselves.

Jane Austen (1775–1817)

O Lord, let us not live to be useless,
for Christ's sake.

John Wesley (1703–91)

✳

I commit myself into the hands of my
Leader, to place me where he wants me in
the battle: I commit myself into the hands
of my Physician, to give me what remedies
he knows are necessary: I commit myself
into his hands, those same dear hands
which bore the cross, that he may lay on
me what cross he sees is best. Lord, give
me grace some day to win the battle,
some day to be made whole by your
goodness, and one day, by the cross,
to gain my crown.

J M Neale (1818–66)

✳

Speak, Lord, for thy servant heareth.
Grant us ears to hear,
Eyes to see,
Wills to obey,
Hearts to love.
Then declare what thou wilt,
Reveal what thou wilt,
Command what thou wilt,
Demand what thou wilt.

Christina Rossetti (1830–94)

My prayers, my God, flow from what
    I am not;
I think thy answers make me
    what I am.
Like weary waves thought follows
    upon thought,
But the still depth beneath is all
    thine own,
And there thou mov'st in paths
    to us unknown.
Out of strange strife thy peace is
    strangely wrought;
If the lion in us pray – thou answerest
    the lamb.

George Macdonald (1824–1905)

*

Take my life, and let it be
Consecrated, Lord, to thee.

Take my moments and my days,
Let them flow in ceaseless praise.

Take my hands and let them move
At the impulse of thy love.

Take my feet and let them be
Swift and beautiful for thee.

Take my voice, and let me sing
Always, only, for my King.

Take my lips and let them be
Filled with messages from thee.

Take my silver and my gold;
Not a mite would I withhold.

Take my intellect, and use
Every power as thou shalt choose.

Take my will, and make it thine;
It shall be no longer mine.

Take my heart; it is thine own;
It shall be thy royal throne.

Take my love; my Lord, I pour
At thy feet its treasure-store.

Take myself, and I will be
Ever, only all for thee.

Frances Ridley Havergal (1836–79)

Here, Lord, is my life.
I place it on the altar today.
Use it as you will.

Albert Schweitzer (1875–1965)

＊

Almighty God, from whom all thoughts of
truth and peace proceed; kindle, we pray
thee, in the hearts of all men the true love
of peace, and guide with thy pure and
peaceable wisdom those who take counsel
for the nations of the earth; that in
tranquillity thy kingdom may go forward,
till the earth be filled with the knowledge
of thy love; through Jesus Christ our Lord.

1928 Proposed Prayer Book
Francis Paget (1851–1911)

＊

O heavenly Father, protect and bless all
things that have breath: guard them from
all evil and let them sleep in peace.

Albert Schweitzer (1875–1965)

✳

When the day returns, call us with morning
faces, and with morning hearts, eager to
labour, happy if happiness be our portion,
and if the day is marked for sorrow, strong
to endure.

Robert Louis Stevenson (1850–94)

✳

Jesus, Master Carpenter of Nazareth, who
on the cross through wood and nails didst
work man's whole salvation: wield well thy
tools in this thy workshop; that we who have
come to thee rough hewn, may by thy hand
be fashioned to a truer beauty and a greater
usefulness, for the honour of thy name.

Toc H Prayers

We give back, to you, O God, those whom
you gave to us. You did not lose them when
you gave them to us, and we do not lose
them by their return to you. Your dear son
has taught us that life is eternal and love
cannot die. So death is only an horizon,
and an horizon is only the limit of our sight.
Open our eyes to see more clearly, and draw
us closer to you that we may know that we
are nearer to our loved ones, who are with
you. You have told us that you are preparing
a place for us: prepare us also for that happy
place, that where you are we may also be
always, O dear Lord of life and death.

Charles Henry Brent (1862–1929)

Grant unto us, O Lord, the royalty of inward happiness and the serenity which comes from living close to thee. Daily renew in us the sense of joy, and let thy eternal Spirit dwell in our souls and bodies, filling every corner of our lives with light and gladness; so that bearing about with us the infection of good courage, we may meet all life's ills or accidents with gallant and high-hearted happiness, giving thee thanks always for all things.

Lucy H M Soulsby (1856–1927)

✳

O God, our loving Father, we pray thee to ever keep us close to thyself, that we may find in thy love our strength and our peace.

William Temple (1881–1944)

✳

Night is drawing nigh.
For all that has been – Thanks!
For all that shall be – Yes!

Dag Hammarskjöld (1905–61)

*

O blessed Jesu Christ, who didst bid all
who carry heavy burdens to come to thee,
refresh us with thy presence and thy power.
Quiet our understandings and give ease to
our hearts, by bringing us close to things
infinite and eternal. Open us to the mind
of God, that in his light we may see light.
And crown thy choice of us to be thy
servants, by making us springs of strength
and joy to all whom we serve.

Evelyn Underhill (1875–1941)

*

O God of many names,
Lover of all nations,
We pray for peace
    in our hearts,
    in our homes,
    in our nations,
    in our world,
The peace of your will,
The peace of our need.

George Appleton (b. 1902)

✳

O thou great Chief, light a candle in my heart, that I may see what is therein, and sweep the rubbish from thy dwelling-place.

An African schoolgirl's prayer (20th century)

✳

Make us worthy, Lord,
to serve our fellow-men
throughout the world who live and die
in poverty or hunger.
Give them, through our hands
this day their daily bread,
and by our understanding love,
give peace and joy.

Mother Teresa of Calcutta

✳

God is what thought cannot better; God
is whom thought cannot reach; God no
thinking can even conceive. Without God,
man can have no being, no reason, no
knowledge, no good desire, naught. Thou,
O God, art what thou art, transcending all.

Eric Milner-White (1884–1964)

✳

O Lord, remember not only the men and women of good will, but also those of ill will. But do not remember all the suffering they have inflicted on us; remember the fruits we have bought, thanks to this suffering – our comradeship, our loyalty, our humility, our courage, our generosity, the greatness of heart which has grown out of all this, and when they come to judgement let all the fruits which we have borne be their forgiveness.

Unknown prisoner in Ravensbruck concentration camp
(20th century)

*

Grant peace and eternal rest to all the departed, but especially to the millions known and unknown who died as prisoners in many lands, victims of the hatred and cruelty of man. May the example of their suffering and courage draw us closer to thee through thine own agony and passion, and thus strengthen us in our desire to serve thee in the sick, the unwanted and the dying wherever we may find them. Give us grace so to spend ourselves for those who are still alive, that we may prove most truly that we have not forgotten those who have died.

Sue Ryder and Leonard Cheshire

*

O Father of all, we pray to thee for those whom we love, but see no longer. Grant them thy peace; let light perpetual shine upon them; and in thy loving wisdom and almighty power work in them the good purpose of thy perfect will; through Jesus Christ our Lord. Amen.

1928 Proposed Prayer Book

＊

Almighty God, Father of all mercies and giver of all comfort: Deal graciously, we pray thee, with those who mourn, that casting every care on thee, they may know the consolation of thy love; through Jesus Christ our Lord. Amen.

1928 Proposed Prayer Book

＊

Death and I are only nodding acquaintances.
We have not been formally introduced
But many times I have noticed
The final encounter
Here in this hospice,
I can truly say
That death has been met with dignity.
Who can divine the thoughts
Of a man in close confrontation?
I can only remember
One particular passing
When a man,
With sustained smile
Pointed out what was for him
Evidently a great light.
Who knows what final revelations
Are received in the last hours?
Lord, grant me a star in the East
As well as a smouldering sunset.

Sidney G Reeman (d. 1975)

*

Remember, O Lord, what thou hast
wrought in us, and not what we deserve;
and as thou has called us to thy service
make us worthy of our calling; through
Jesus Christ our Lord. Amen.

1928 Proposed Prayer Book
Leonine Sacramentary

＊

I find prayer so powerful
That I need but one:
Heavenly Father
Grant me the wisdom
To see the good
In everyone
And everything.
You know my needs:
I do not need to ask.
I appreciate your gifts.
Amen.

James Haylock Eyre

Come, Holy Spirit, give us hearts of peace
and warmth which can serve as a refuge for
those who suffer. Come help us to be
present to one another.

Jean Vanier

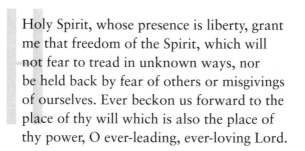

Holy Spirit, whose presence is liberty, grant
me that freedom of the Spirit, which will
not fear to tread in unknown ways, nor
be held back by fear of others or misgivings
of ourselves. Ever beckon us forward to the
place of thy will which is also the place of
thy power, O ever-leading, ever-loving Lord.

George Appleton (b. 1902)

Self-offering

Almighty God, Father, Son,
   and Holy Ghost,
to me the least of saints,
to me allow that I may keep a door
   in Paradise.
That I may keep even the small door,
the farthest, darkest, coldest door,
the door that is least used,
the stiffest door.
If so it be in thine house, O God,
if so it be that I can see thy glory even afar,
and hear thy voice,
and know that I am with thee, O God.

St Columba (521–97)

O Lord our God, grant us grace to desire thee with our whole heart, so that, desiring thee, we may seek and find thee; and so finding thee, may love thee; and loving thee may hate those sins which separate us from thee, for the sake of Jesus Christ.

St Anselm (1033–1109)

*

God, of your goodness give me yourself for you are sufficient for me. I cannot properly ask anything less, to be worthy of you. If I were to ask less, I should always be in want. In you alone do I have all.

Julian of Norwich (1342–1413)

*

O Lord Jesus Christ, who created and
redeemed me, and hast brought me unto
that which now I am, thou knowest what
thou wouldst do with me; do with me
according to thy will; for thy tender
mercy's sake.

King Henry VI (1421–72)

✳

O Lord Jesus Christ,
who art the way, the truth and the life;
we pray thee not to suffer us
to stray from thee, who art the way;
not to distrust thee who art the truth,
nor to rest on any other than thee,
who art the life.
Teach us what to believe,
what to do and wherein to take our rest.

Erasmus (1467–1536)

✳

Teach us, good Lord, to serve thee
    as thou deservest:
to give and not to count the cost;
to fight and not to heed the wounds;
to toil and not to seek for rest;
to labour and not to ask for any reward
save that of knowing that we do thy will.

Ignatius of Loyola (1491–1556)

*

O Lord, my God, I have hope in thee;
O my dear Jesus, set me free.
Though hard the chains that fasten me
And sore my lot, yet I long for thee.
I languish and groaning bend my knee,
Adoring, imploring, O set me free.

Mary Queen of Scots (1542–87)
(on the eve of her execution)

*

Batter my heart, three personed God;
    for, you
As yet but knock, breathe, shine,
    and seek to mend;
That I may rise, and stand,
    o'erthrow me, and bend
Your force to break, blow,
    burn and make me new.
I, like an usurped town, to another due,
Labour to admit you, but oh, to no end,
Reason your viceroy in me,
    me should defend,
But is captived, and proves weak or untrue.
Yet dearly I love you,
    and would be loved fain,
But am betrothed unto your enemy,
Divorce me, untie, or break
    that knot again,
Take me to you, imprison me, for I
Except you enthral me, never shall be free,
Nor ever chaste, except you ravish me.

John Donne (1571–1631)

✳

Open thou mine eyes that I may see
Incline my heart that I may desire
Order my steps that I may follow
The way of thy commandments.

Lancelot Andrewes (1555–1626)

✳

My Lord, I have nothing to do in this world
but to seek and serve thee. I have nothing to
do with my heart and its affections but to
breathe after thee. I have nothing to do
with my tongue and pen but to speak to
thee and for thee, and to publish thy glory
and thy will.

Richard Baxter (1615–91)

✳

Lord, let Thy glory be my end,
Thy word my rule,
and then Thy will be done.

King Charles I (1600–49)

✳

O heavenly Father, touch and penetrate and
shake and awaken the inmost depth and
centre of my soul, that all that is within me
may cry and call to you. Strike the flinty
rock of my heart that the water of eternal
life may spring up in it. Oh break open the
gates of the great deep in my soul, that
your light may shine in upon me, that
I may enter into your Kingdom of light
and love, and in your light see light.

William Law (1686–1761)

✳

O God, the Father of the forsaken, who dost teach us that love towards man is the bond of perfectness and the imitation of thyself: open our eyes and touch our hearts that we may see and do the things which belong to our peace. Strengthen us in the work which we have undertaken; give us wisdom, perseverance, faith and zeal; and in thine own time and according to thy pleasure prosper the issue; for the love of thy Son Jesus Christ our Lord.

Lord Shaftesbury (1801–85)

Guide us, teach us, and strengthen us,
O Lord, we beseech thee, until we become
such as thou wouldst have us be, pure,
gentle, truthful, high-minded, courteous,
generous, able, dutiful and useful; for thy
honour and glory.

Charles Kingsley (1819–75)

*

O Lord, support us all the day long of this
troublous life, until the shadows lengthen,
the evening comes, the fever of life is over
and our work on earth is done; then Lord,
in Thy mercy grant us safe lodging, a holy
rest, and peace at the last.

1928 Proposed Prayer Book
Cardinal Newman (1801–90)

*

Holy Spirit, coming so silently,
giving life and refreshment
    and beauty everywhere;
coming in a way none can understand;
coming invisibly;
coming in the night of affliction;
may your peace dwell in my heart,
may your strength invigorate me,
may your love kindle my whole being,
to love him who first loved me.

Lord, whether I am good or bad
I am always yours.
If you won't have me, who will?
If you take no notice, who will care for me?
Your forgiveness far outweighs
    my wickedness;
your love is much deeper than the depth
    of my sin.
Lord, whatever kind of a person I am,
I am always yours.

J M Neale (1818–66)

I believe in the sun even when it is
not shining.
I believe in love even when I cannot feel it.
I believe in God, even when he is silent.

Jewish prisoner (1940s)

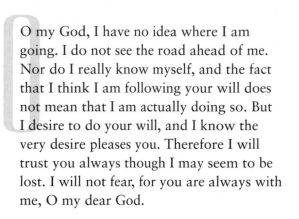

O my God, I have no idea where I am
going. I do not see the road ahead of me.
Nor do I really know myself, and the fact
that I think I am following your will does
not mean that I am actually doing so. But
I desire to do your will, and I know the
very desire pleases you. Therefore I will
trust you always though I may seem to be
lost. I will not fear, for you are always with
me, O my dear God.

Thomas Merton (1915–68)

Since today is a new day
I will begin again
With Jesus Christ, my Lord.

Bob Knight

✳

Give us
A pure heart
That we may see Thee,
A humble heart
That we may hear Thee,
A heart of love
That we may serve Thee,
A heart of faith
That we may live Thee,
Thou whom I do not know
But whose I am.

Dag Hammarskjöld (1905–61)

✳

TRUSTING

May God himself, the God of peace, make you holy through and through, and keep you sound in spirit, soul and body, free of any fault when our Lord Jesus Christ comes.

I Thessalonians 5.23

Watch thou, O Lord, with those who wake, or watch, or weep tonight, and give thine angels charge over those who sleep. Tend thy sick ones, O Lord Christ; rest thy weary ones; bless thy dying ones; soothe thy suffering ones; pity thine afflicted ones; shield thy joyous ones, and all for thy love's sake.

St Augustine (354–430)

I bind unto myself today
The power of God to hold and lead
His eye to watch, his might to stay
His ear to hearken to my need:
The wisdom of my God to teach,
His hand to guide, his shield to ward,
The word of God to give me speech,
His heavenly host to be my guard.

St Patrick (389–461)

*

Be thou a bright flame before me,
Be thou a guiding star above me,
Be thou a smooth path below me,
Be thou a kindly shepherd behind me,
Today, tonight and for ever.

St Columba (521–97)

*

Be present, O merciful God, and protect us
through the silent hours of this night, so
that we who are wearied by the changes
and chances of this fleeting world may
repose upon thine eternal changelessness;
through Jesus Christ our Lord.

1928 Proposed Prayer Book
Gelasian Sacramentary (7th century)

✳

Christ is the morning star who
when the darkness of the world is past
brings to his saints
the promise of the light of life
and opens everlasting day.

Venerable Bede (673–735)

✳

May the right hand of the Lord keep us ever
in old age, the grace of Christ continually
defend us from the enemy. O Lord, direct
our heart in the way of peace; through
Jesus Christ our Lord.

Bishop Aedelwald (8th century)

Eternal Light, shine into our hearts,
Eternal Goodness, deliver us from evil,
Eternal Power, be our support,
Eternal Wisdom, scatter the darkness
    of our ignorance.
Eternal Pity, have mercy on us;
that with all our heart and mind
and soul and strength
we may seek thy face and be brought by
thine infinite mercy to thy holy presence;
through Jesus Christ our Lord.

Alcuin of York (735–804)

Into thy hands, O Father and Lord, we commend our souls and bodies, our parents and our homes, friends and servants, neighbours and kindred, our benefactors and brethren departed, all folk rightly believing, and all who need thy pity and protection. Light us all with thy holy grace, and suffer us never to be separated from thee, O Lord in Trinity, God everlasting.

Edmund Rich (1170–1240)

Do you wish to understand
    your Lord's meaning?

Understand truly: Love was His meaning.
Who revealed it to you? Love.
What did He show you? Love.
Why did He show it? For love.

Hold firmly to this and you will learn and
know more of this. But you will never know
or learn anything other than this, ever.

It is God's eternal will that we remain
secure in love and peaceful and restful, as
He is to us. Just as He is to us, so it is His
will we should be to ourselves and to our
fellow Christians. Amen.

Julian of Norwich (1342–1413)

*

Preserve us, O Lord, while waking, and
guard us while sleeping, that awake we may
watch with Christ, and asleep we may rest
in peace.

1928 Proposed Prayer Book
Compline Anthem

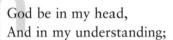

God be in my head,
And in my understanding;

God be in my eyes,
And in my looking;

God be in my mouth,
And in my speaking;

God be in my heart,
And in my thinking;

God be at my end,
And at my departing.

Pynson's Horae (1514)

Christ has no body now on earth but yours,
no hands but yours, no feet but yours;
yours are the eyes through which to look at
Christ's compassion to the world, yours are
the feet with which he is to go about doing
good, and yours are the hands with which
he is to bless us now.

St Teresa of Avila (1515–82)

*

O Lord our God,
give us by thy Holy Spirit
a willing heart and a ready hand
to use all thy gifts to thy praise and glory;
through Jesus Christ our Lord.

Thomas Cranmer (1489–1556)

*

Lord God, when you call your servants to
endeavour any great matter, grant us also
to know that it is not the beginning, but
the continuing of the same, until it be
thoroughly finished, which yields the true
glory; through him who, for the finishing
of your work, laid down his life for us, our
Redeemer, Jesus Christ.

*Prayer based on the words of
Sir Francis Drake (1540–96)*

*

To God the Father, who loved us and made
us accepted in the Beloved: To God the Son,
who loved us and loosed us from our sins
by his own blood: To God the Holy Spirit,
who sheds the love of God abroad in our
hearts: To the one true God, be all love and
all glory for time and eternity. Amen.

Thomas Ken (1637–1711)

*

God, Sovereign Lord of all,
you loved the world so much
that you gave your only Son,
born of a woman, born under the law,
to suffer, die and rise again,
so that everyone who has faith in him
through the indwelling of the
    Holy Spirit
may advance in wisdom and
    your favour,
possessing eternal life.
This is my faith.
Help me where faith falls short.

Lancelot Andrewes (1555–1626)

*

Glory to thee, my God, this night
For all the blessings of the light;
Keep me, O keep me, King of Kings,
Beneath thine own almighty wings.

Thomas Ken (1637–1711)

Bring us, O Lord God, at our last
awakening into the house and gate of
heaven, to enter into that gate and dwell in
that house, where there shall be no darkness
nor dazzling, but one equal light; no noise
nor silence, but one equal music; no fears
nor hopes, but one equal possession; no
ends, nor beginnings, but one equal
eternity; in the habitations of thy glory
and dominion, world without end.

John Donne (1571–1631)

Go forth upon thy journey from this world,
O Christian soul, in the peace of him in
whom thou hast believed, in the name
of God the Father, who created thee, in the
name of Jesus Christ, who suffered for
thee, in the name of the Holy Spirit,
who strengthened thee. May angels
and archangels and all the armies of the
heavenly host, come to meet thee, may all
the saints of God welcome thee, may thy
portion this day be in gladness and peace,
thy dwelling in Paradise, Go forth upon thy
journey, O Christian Soul.

Prayer for the dying

✳

God to enfold me,
God to surround me,
God in my speaking,
God in my thinking.
God in my sleeping,
God in my waking,
God in my watching,
God in my hoping.
God in my life,
God in my lips,
God in my soul,
God in my heart.
God in my sufficing,
God in my slumber,
God in mine ever-living soul,
God in mine eternity.

Carmina Gadelica (19th century)

INDEX OF FIRST LINES

INDEX OF AUTHORS
AND SOURCES

ACKNOWLEDGEMENTS

The compiler and publisher gratefully
acknowledge permission to reproduce copyright
material in this anthology. Every effort has been
made to trace and contact copyright holders. If
there are any inadvertent omissions we
apologise to those concerned and will ensure
that a suitable acknowledgement is made at
the next reprint.

The Archbishops' Council of the Church of
England: from *The Alternative Service Book
1980* (pp. 24, 30); from the *1928 Proposed
Prayer Book* (pp. 50, 59, 61, 71, 77, 81).
Cassells plc: from *The Prayer Manual* edited by
Frederick MacNutt (p. 53).
Darton, Longman and Todd: from *Beyond All
Pain* edited by Cicely Saunders (pp. 60, 61).
Faber and Faber Ltd.: from *Markings* by Dag
Hammarskjöld (pp. 54, 76).
Victor Gollancz: from *God of a Hundred Names*
(pp. 49, 50).
Hodder and Stoughton: from *Blessings* edited by
Mary Craig (p. 58).
International Committee on English in the
Liturgy, Inc.: from *The Sunday Missal* (p. 28).
Oxford University Press: from *The Oxford Book*

of Prayer edited by George Appleton (pp. 55, 64); from *A Diary of Private Prayer* by John Baillie (p. 23).

SPCK: from *In the Silence of the Heart* (p. 56); from *My God, My Glory* by Eric Milner-White (p. 56).

Toc H: (pp. 51, 74).

Extracts from *The Book of Common Prayer (1662)*, the rights in which are vested in the Crown, are reproduced by permission of the Crown's Patentee, Cambridge University Press (pp. 13, 19, 21, 22, 26, 29, 33(2), 43, 44). Bible texts are used with permission from *The Revised English Bible* © 1989 Oxford and Cambridge University Presses.